ISBN: 978-0-359-45598-0

This book is available on www.lulu.com and www.amazon.com, at bookstores, including Sun Dial Books on Chincoteague, or by direct request to the author.

To contact the author regarding permissions, speaking engagements, etc. email LoisSzymanski@hotmail.com

Printed in the United States of AmericaOther Books by Lois Szymanski:
****
Chincoteague Pony Tales

Chincoteague Pony Tales – Volume II
Surfer Dude
Your Chincoteague Pony Foal's First Year
Wild Colt
The True Story of Sea Feather
The True Story of Miracle Man
Chincoteague Ponies: Untold Tales
Out of the Sea: Today's Chincoteague Pony

Thank you to **cliparting.com**.

Meet this orphan foal on page 79.

Photo Courtesy of Hunter Leonard

Chincoteague Pony Tales III

Lois Szymanski

© 2007 Julie Childs

Meet Prince Snipperdoodle on page 71!

Forward

Established in 1943, the Chincoteague National Wildlife Refuge on Assateague Island has more than 14,000 acres of beach, dunes, marsh and mud, loblolly pines and maritime forests. The wild ponies who live on the Refuge are owned by the Chincoteague Volunteer Fire Company whose saltwater cowboys work tirelessly to care for them.

Those of us who follow the ponies love knowing their backstories, but we also love hearing where they are today. That is what this book series is all about – sharing the stories that unfold on the refuge, and stories born after the foal goes home.

None of what I share would happen without the Chincoteague Volunteer Fire Company. It is the hard work of their members that make it possible.

The fire company drops bales of hay in the winter when wind and ice, snow and cold arrive. They fill water troughs when freshwater ponds freeze over. They round the ponies up in the spring and the fall for health care and shots. They wrestle foals into the sale ring annually on the last Thursday of July, to control the wild pony population. More times than we realize, these volunteers leave the comfort of their homes to slog through mud and marsh, fight biting flies and swarms of mosquitoes the likes of which you've never seen, to rescue a pony in trouble.

I hope you enjoy the stories I've tracked down, and if you have a story of your own to share, please let me know. I am always looking for the next story for the next volume of Chincoteague Pony Tales!

©2018 Lois Szymanski

Baby Bandit – Read his story on page 45!

Contents

Sugar and Spice

This is the story of Ella's foal, as shared with me by pony committee member and saltwater cowboy, John "Hunter" Leonard.

Hunter said it was a warm spring day in 2016 when he heard about a foal in trouble. Friend, Cindy Faith had been working a bus trek, taking Road Scholars north, to see the pony herds, when a colt came through the bushes on the side of the road, all alone. Realizing the implications of a foal all alone, Cindy called the fire company to make a report

©2016 DSC Photography

Hunter arrived shortly after, with several pony committee members along. There, they found a sweet little chestnut filly with a blaze, standing alone, along the fence-line.

"She was friendly and inquisitive and let us come right over to her," Hunter said. "We had to retain her while waiting for a trailer to get over there, and after two hours [of waiting], we were getting tired of holding her, so we tied her to the back of the pickup truck, and she stayed there."

Hunter laughed as he recalled how the foal could go 40 to 50 feet out.

"She only wigged out once. She seemed to understand that she wasn't going to go anywhere."

The foal – at about two weeks old – was too young to wean. The cowboys loaded her onto the trailer and took her to the Leonard farm.

"We put her in the fence. She walked around, and then she drank a little water," Hunter said, noting that that it's not normal for them to drink water at this young age, so she had to be thirsty. "We went out to get some Foal All, a powdered milk for foals. It's not the best, but we figured she'd already gotten the colostrum, since she wasn't a brand new foal."

The filly was amicable and easy to handle, that is, until they tried to get her into a stall.

"She kicked me hard in the leg and put a nice dent in my iPhone," Hunter recalled. "We'd found her around 11 or noon and it was now about 5 p.m., so she had to be getting hungry. We had the milk and it was warm, but the bottle we were using had a nipple for a calf bottle, which is too long. It went too far into her mouth to drink, so we gave her some like we would drink, right from the bottle [without a lid] and we were able to get some into her. We thought we'd have to do an all night shift, every two hours, but then I gave her a bucket of milk. It's very unusual for a foal to drink out of a bucket, but darned if she didn't do it. I hung up the bucket and she drank it all. She belted it down. It was amazing!"

By then, it was at least 6 p.m. Hunter said he was beat, but he sat down and pulled up DSC Photography on Facebook. Darcy and Steve Cole hike at least five times a week to record foal births, often more, documenting them with photos on their Facebook page for everyone who loves the ponies.

"I started scrolling through Darcy's pictures, and I found three pictures from a long way away. The mare was Ella and I thought her foal looked like this one. There was another, but the blaze wasn't quite right on that one.

©2016 DSC Photography

Hunter picked up the phone to call pony committee chairman, Bobby Lapin and they made a plan to try to reunite the foal and its dam in the morning.

The next day found the pair heading north, into the muddy piping plover area, with Bobby driving his truck and several others along, including Charlene – a Chincoteague Wildlife Refuge employee.

"It's dangerous in that area," Hunter recalled. "He almost got stuck, but he made it through, and we found Ella not far away, with Prince's herd.

The mosquitoes were horrible, buzzing around their heads like a swarm of hornets, but the group plodded on with the foal in tow, a lasso around its neck.

"Most of the time when you approach a band, they are inquisitive and then, they decide whether to move off or just stand still. Sometimes they don't care. Sometimes they do," Hunter said. "When we approached the band, Ella came right over and nuzzled her foal, but she didn't drink. We were thinking… *oh no, maybe too much time has passed*, but we could tell that this was her mother."

When the band walked off, the group wasn't sure what to do. What if she didn't accept the foal back? So, they followed, the lasso still around her neck. They walked and walked, with the mare continually turning to check on her filly, occasionally nuzzling her.

"We finally got to the point where we knew they were going to keep going," Hunter said. "We didn't want to take the lasso off, because if we took it off and she didn't keep up, we would never catch her again out there in the wild. Finally, Charlene said, 'You might as well take it off and see what happens.'"

Hunter said that's when Bobby removed the lasso, and off the herd went, disappearing into the brush and trees.

"Sometimes you just have to have faith that things will be okay," Hunter said. And that is what they did that day.

When the foal and her dam came in together at Pony Penning, Hunter said it touched him.

"It was a good feeling, just knowing they made it. "They looked so good," he recalled.

Richard Killian Photo

Photo Courtesy Country Lane Farm

Seeing that sweet little filly in the auction ring in 2016 was like witnessing a blessing. Hunter and his crew had surely saved this filly's life.

It was good to watch the foal heading home with his new family. The Schauders purchased Ella's filly, and one more. They own and run a show stable called Country Lane Farm in Connecticut.

"We hadn't intended to buy two," Christina Schauder said. "My youngest daughter [Avery] fell in love with the chestnut. She kept an eye on it all week, and she told me, 'This one is speaking to me.' The chestnut was hanging out with the palomino all week. We later learned [from Darcy Cole] they were siblings, born on the same day."

Christina said both ponies are under saddle now, Ella's foal, and Rainbow Delight's foal. Each has a personality that is very much her own.

"They are both amazing," she said. "They are jumping, trail riding. and walk, trot, cantering now. They have so much common sense, and they are not mare-ish at all."

The family named the palomino pinto, Sugar and they named Ella's foal Spice.

"Spice moves well and jumps well. She is amazing in the ring. And they both love to jump. If you put them in an empty ring with jumps, they will jump them with nobody on their backs."

We love it when everything turns out well, and in this case it surely did. Sugar and Spice truly are everything nice!

Photo Courtesy of Country Lane Farm

Find Country Lane Farm online at: www.countrylanefarm.com.

Angels Among Us

Many know the story of how a cancer survivor with a heart of gold helped dreams come true for two young girls who were bidding on foals at the 1995 pony penning auction. It is the story of Carollynn Suplee, the cancer survivor who – for the eight years she survived cancer – purchased a pony foal for a child or a buyback annually as a way of "giving back for another year of life." Carollynn and the amazing example she set were the inspiration for the nonprofit, The Feather Fund (www.featherfund.net).

One of the ponies Carollynn purchased was for a young boy named Matt Loveland, in 1999.

Matt, came to the auction that year with a handful of money and a dream, but the prices were high, and his savings fell

Photo Courtesy Matt Loveland

short. Then Carollynn and her husband, Ed stepped in, and a dream came true. Matt took home a black and white pinto colt that he named Ace of Spades. Even back then, Matt said he dreamed of being a saltwater cowboy one day.

As the years passed, Matt outgrew his pony and passed it on to a neighborhood friend, but he continued to dream of riding in the roundup. And every year at Pony Penning, Matt hung out with the cowboys he'd come to know.

Over the years, Matt married and had a son of his own, but he still dreamed of riding in a roundup. Then, in 2019, Matt purchased a beautiful bay American Quarter Horse named Pepper, one he believed was smart enough and solid enough to take to the strenuous week-long roundup, with mucky marshes and "herds" of mosquitoes. In preparation, he competed in cattle penning events, continuing to ride and dream of that day.

Then, it came – in the spring of 2019 – the call asking him if he would like to ride in the pony penning roundup.

"My family and I have become really good friends with a handful of the other riders," Matt said, counting his blessings. "If it wasn't for them none of it would have happened, nor would I know what I was doing out there on the marsh."

On the Saturday of Pony Penning 2019, Matt rode in the south roundup. I remember watching him and Pepper at the south pens. I don't know if I'd ever seen him looking so happy.

"The best feeling was that first morning, loading my horse on the trailer with the boys," he told me. "After so many times watching everyone tack up and load up while I was left behind, that moment was the best."

On Sunday, Matt mounted Pepper to ride in the north roundup. I saw him again on Monday, helping bring the ponies into the south pens after the annual Beachwalk. That's when the northern herds, surrounded by saltwater cowboys are walked down the beach to the southern pens against a backdrop of ocean and sunrise. It's a beautiful sight, silhouettes before a surging ocean, lit by a ball fire in the sky.

"The best sight was walking the north herd over the dunes and down the beach, just so peaceful," Matt said.

I chatted with Matt a few times throughout the week. He sent messages from time to time while anticipation built for the pony swim that would take place on Wednesday. It would be the culmination of his dream. Still, Matt worried.

"I hope Pepper steps onto the barge," he told me.

I understood his concern. For a horse, stepping onto a strange floating barge is asking a lot. But, that night, Matt sent me a photo of a feather.

"Walked out my room [and] in the middle of the hallway sat this little beauty," he wrote in the message. "This will be riding in my pocket tomorrow!"

I smiled when I read the message. Carollynn always said feathers were a sign for her that things would be okay. She loved Psalm 91: verse 4, which tells us how the Lord will cover you with feathers and protect you. She was sending a sign to Matt that she was there, watching him ride.

Swim day arrived. It turned out, there had been no need for worry. Pepper took it all in stride, never hesitating when asked to step onto the barge. He did all that was asked of him. It was surreal for Matt, who said, on that day, there was a moment in time when he felt a spiritual presence.

"I remember the ponies running in the water, splashing water all over, [and then] riding through the mud and feeling like my grandfather and Carollynn were watching over," he later told me.

My daughter, Shannon and I had risen early. For the first time ever, we were going to see the swim from a boat. We'd signed up for Captain Dan's Around the Island Cruises, along with several of our best friends. Over the years, Captain Dan, had become a friend we knew we could count on, and on this day he did not disappoint.

The ponies plunged into the water, making the swim early in the day. We saw Matt on the barge, and then lost sight of him for a bit. Then, there he was standing on the point of the marsh alongside two other cowboys on horseback.

"He's texting," I said, laughing. But then my

Photo Courtesy Matt Loveland

phone bonged, and I realized he was messaging me. He'd sent a photo of Pepper's hooves planted in the mucky marsh. Right between the big bay's front hooves laid a feather.

A chill passed over me. I had no doubt that Carollynn was there, making sure he got her message. She was seeing his dream come true.

We laughed and watched the ponies graze along the shoreline. We knew the cowboys were resting them before the parade down Main Street and then into the pens at the carnival grounds where the foals would be auctioned the next day.

As we watched, my phone bonged again. It was Karen Stannard, a friend from Connecticut. She'd sent a photo of the sky over the swim. Before I could even look up, her photo took my breath away. Two perfect feathers hovered in the sky above. The clouds had arranged themselves into a stunningly perfect picture.

I held up my phone.

©2019 Karen Stannard

"Look at this!" I told my daughter and our friends on the boat, sharing the photo. How had we missed it?

Tears filled my eyes. But there was more to come. Other friends were sending photos. We saw how, as the feather clouds drifted apart, the sun had sent rays of light through them, creating a sundog – a rainbow in the clouds. My heart pounded as I stared at the affirmation. I could just picture Carollynn up there, working so hard to rearrange the clouds. She was letting Matt know that she was with him. She was seeing his dream come true – a dream that had started with her gift of a tiny foal on Pony Penning day, many years before.

No one can tell me that angels do not exist. I will not hear them. What I do hear - loud and clear - are messages like this one, sent from above.

On Chincoteague and Assateague, messages like this are not uncommon. Maybe it is part of the reason we have all fallen in love with Chincoteague and Assateague islands. Sometimes it feels like magic hovers in the air, all around us. But maybe it isn't magic at all. Maybe it's all orchestrated by angels. In this case, I feel certain it was.

Gingersnap

So many of us were devastated by the loss of our favorite island stallion, Surfer Dude in 2015. It was expected, because he had aged, but that didn't lessen the blow. For some, his loss spurred the purchase of a foal. Afterall, it would be the last time anyone could take home a Surfer Dude baby. Joyce Westbury was one of those. Even though the Chincoteague resident wasn't ready to bring a foal home, she said losing Surfer Dude was a call to action.

"As I was sitting at the auction, I was thinking that maybe I would bid on a buyback the following year when I turned 65," Joyce recalled. "Then it hit me that there were never going to be any more Surfer Dude foals."

Just after, a tiny chestnut buyback filly came into the ring. She was a daughter of Surfer Dude. Joyce said that suddenly, the only thing that mattered was bidding on the filly - even though she had not discussed this with her husband.

"I was so blessed to win the bid! I couldn't believe it!" Joyce said. "I remember going up to pay for her and [fire company publicity chair] Denise Bowden giving me a hug and thanking me. I looked at her and told her that now I had to go home and tell my husband."

Joyce named the filly Surfer's Shining Star, including both Surfer's name and the name of the filly's dam, Elusive Star. She nicknamed her

Gingersnap. That is the name most know her by.

Gingersnap and her dam, Elusive Star in the wild.
Photo by Darcy & Steve Cole

"She was so sweet," Joyce said. "She just reminded me of a cookie and her color reminded me of a Gingersnap."

Gingersnap spent her first winter at the carnival grounds, as all buybacks, do. This gives them a strong foundation to grow on once they are released into the wild in the spring. It also gave Joyce a chance to visit the filly often throughout the fall and winter.

Joyce believes having Gingersnap in her life was part of God's plan, because just a few months later – on September 2nd - she lost her husband very suddenly. Watching Gingersnap thrive on the carnival grounds, loving her, and watching her adapt to life on the island after she was released surely helped Joyce during the long hard healing process.

©2015 Lois Szymanski

Loving a buyback is a beautiful thing, but it does not come without a little stress. Once they are released into the wild, anything can happen, and for Gingersnap, happen it did.

Hunter Leonard shared how Gingersnap was found, badly injured, when she was just two years old.

"I believe it was around Memorial Day or just after that year," he said. "We had some friends along and had gone out on a cruise. I was sailing up towards Cherry Hill Bay. That area is where you come to the end of Chincoteague and you look across the marsh. I could see a horse standing there right next to our clubhouse at Red Eye. She was next to the water.

Right away, my friend noticed that something was wrong. She wasn't moving much, and when we looked, we realized that she had two massive, baseball-sized gashes in both front legs."

Hunter said Gingersnap was calm, but her location was at least a mile from the road, too far to walk her to meet a trailer, especially with the cuts.

"I had cruises to do. I was scheduled to work, so I got the troops moving," he recalled. "I called some of the cowboys and my dad, and I dropped the vet off with her, right out on the marsh."

Hunter smiled before continuing. "When I came back on the next tour - about two hours later - I see a bunch of cowboys coming toward us on a boat, and when we got closer, I noticed they looked kind of giddy. Then I see her, right there on the floor of the boat!" He laughed.

It turns out, the cowboys had tried walking her toward a trailer, but quickly realized it truly was too far. So instead, they rolled her over, right into the boat.

"She was so small. They were all smiling while holding her there. She rode along, as calm as could be. I could tell they thought it was funny," Hunter said.

The boat carried Gingersnap to the Leonard's Chincoteague Pony Farm on the north end of the island, where she was able to walk to the barn by herself. Her cuts were scabbed over but clearly infected underneath.

"We thought maybe she had been chased into the bushes," Hunter said. "It was terrible. The infection was deep in both legs."

Hunter said, every night, after arriving home from work, he'd go to her stall to treat her.

"I'd put her in the chute, wet some sterile gauze pads and clean it out. She would turn around and nip at me or watch me, but she only tried to cow kick me one time," he said, adding that this was his nightly routine for about four weeks.

"Every day, you could see her healing a little bit more," Hunter's wife, Rebekah said. "It was crazy how fast she healed. She's sweet though, and I loved having her at the farm. She would lay her head right on my shoulder."

"She loved grain, Hunter said. "Man, did she ever love grain." I called her Ginger for the longest time. I'd call, 'Ginger!' and she'd come running."

Darcy Cole shook her head when she recalled seeing her on the day she was injured. "I did not think she was coming back from that," she said.

And Hunter agreed. "It was really bad," he said.

The saltwater cowboys who work to care for the ponies we love - while allowing them to still live wild – are faced with a real balancing act, yet they do it so well. It is only because of them that Gingersnap was able to survive. She truly was, and still is, Surfer's Shining Star.

I remember the sunny day in early June when Gingersnap was released again in the north. I was out on a cruise with Captain Dan and we came upon her, grazing in lush marsh grasses out on a point that jutted out from the island, into the water. We knew of course that she had been on the Leonard Farm to be treated for cuts, so it was a surprise to see her there. Captain Dan explained how she had must have just been released.

A few days later, it was reported that Gingersnap had joined one of the herds on the island. She thrived, and then, in 2019, sweet Gingersnap had her first foal. That is a story all in itself, and you can read about that in the next chapter.

©2017 Lois Szymanski

Gingersnap – the pony who rode in a boat. This was taken on the day she was released, after recuperating from her injuries.

Snickerdoodle

Living on Chincoteague and watching her buyback mare Gingersnap grow has filled Joyce Westbury with joy. But she's experienced worry and anticipation, too, the overwhelming anticipation she felt while waiting for the mare to have her first foal in the spring of 2019. I think, perhaps, she knew even back then, that she would fall in love the foal, no matter what the color, size or sex. Afterall, this would be Gingersnap's baby, and a grand foal of Surfer Dude, as well!

"I couldn't wait to see this little filly up close and to watch her destiny unfold," Joyce said, describing how she felt when she heard her mare had given birth. "In the back of my mind I always hoped that she would be picked as a buyback or that the Chincoteague Legacy Group would be interested in her, or even one of the Feather Fund kids. That way I had the chance of keeping tabs on her."

When that did not happen, Joyce found it hard to let go of the love she already had for the little palomino pinto foal.

"When I got to see her close up during Pony Penning there was something about her that intrigued me," Joyce said. "She was just another palomino pinto filly, but I fell so deeply in love with her.

Joyce said she thought about buying her, but she knew she couldn't offer her a very good life. Two miniature horses already occupied her Chincoteague yard – not big enough for a full sized Chincoteague Pony.

"I wanted her so bad!" she said.

© 2019 Joyce Westbury

Gingersnap and her filly 2019.

Friendship and destiny were about to collide. After her husband passed in 2015, Joyce had become good friends with Mary Morrow on Facebook. She'd lost her husband about the same time.

"When she and her girls would come to Pony Penning each year, we would always hook up at least for a little bit," Joyce said. "This year, we were hanging out at the carnival grounds the night before the auction and talking - of course - about the foals. I jokingly said I would buy Gingersnap's foal and she could go live on Mary's farm. I remember Mary and Julie looking at each other and then at me and saying, 'Yes! She could!' I stared at them both and it took me a couple of minutes to realize they were not kidding."

Mary also remembered that moment.

"Joyce was practically in tears about wanting to buy her, so I said, 'Well, if you want to buy her, we could keep her for you.' I remember that she said, 'Are you serious?' and I said, "Yes!'"

Joyce said she did a lot of praying that night.

"After tossing and turning and praying and looking at my finances all night, I knew I had to bid on her," she said. "I had $3,400 to do this, so off I went to win her."

Auction morning dawned sunny and warm. Joyce settled into her lawn chair to wait, heart pounding, surrounded by friends. She didn't have to wait long, because Snickerdoodle was number two in the auction, coming out before Joyce had time to think.

"As soon as I saw her, I jumped up and started bidding," she said. "It was probably a stupid thing to have done. I should have been a little more discreet!" She laughed.

"Well the bidding went back and forth between me and someone else who I never saw. It got to $3,400 and my heart stopped. I couldn't go any higher. But the other person didn't bid again, so I won her and then I just burst into tears!"

Joyce said she will never forget that moment. Surely it was destiny, with the filly selling for the exact amount she had to spend.

The next day, Snickerdoodle was loaded onto the trailer to go home with the Morrows. Then, that fall, Mary surprised Joyce by bringing Snickerdoodle to Chincoteague to visit on the weekend of fall roundup.

Since, then, Joyce has visited the Morrow farm several times. She said she feels blessed to have a friend like Mary in her life, and she believes it all is truly the work of God.

"Even though I wish I could see her all of the time, she couldn't have a

© 2019 Mary Morrow

© 2019 Mary Morrow

better home or family to take care of her," Joyce said. "God continues to work in my life, giving me the desires of my heart."

Mary laughs as if she knows it was meant to be.

"We sure do love her!" she said.

And who wouldn't? After all, she is a piece of the wind and sky, and the grand foal of a stallion we all have loved.

Sweet Tea

The year that Surfer Dude passed, was a hard one for many pony-lovers. Darlene Brennan remembers watching the reports unfold on Facebook, and the sinking feeling of knowing that he was gone. That's when they made a plan to be there when his last foals were auctioned off.

"We saw Surf Queen come in alone, and we knew that Surfer Dude had probably died," she said. "In the next few months, his last foals would be born. People started talking about being able to buy one of his last foals as a buyback, and in a few weeks a group was created [The Chincoteague Legacy Group] with the goal of purchasing one of his last foals as a buyback. Our family contributed money. My grandchildren Christopher, Phillip, Nicolette, Isabella, and Maxx wanted to be part of the group. They each gave money to help us reach our dream. We decided we would attend all the events of pony week including the auction. The kids were excited to come to Chincoteague for a week of pony fun."

Darlene said they attended the south and north roundups and the beach walk. Hunter Leonard shared the story of something special that happened while he was riding in that north roundup.

"We get to the wash flats and we see this baby that is just lagging behind," Hunter said. "He was going as hard as he could go but could barely keep up. We made a mental note of it, and then we got to where we funnel really hard and we see this rustling in the bushes. Cody got off his horse and he said, "There's a baby in there!" Sure enough, there was this little chestnut filly."

They cowboys wondered what to do. They didn't have the gator along and were too far out to get the truck. That's when cowboy, Justin Lewis picked her up and draped her over the front of his saddle, riding that foal in, all the way to the corral. There, someone gave the filly sweet tea from a McDonald's cup, a little bit of sugar, before releasing her in the pen, where she quickly found her mama.

©2015 Barbara Bowden - Firewifey352 Photography

It was a memory that the cowboys will cling to forever, because Justin lost his life not long after in a tragic car accident.

Darlene said they saw the foal come in. Her family was spending a lot of time together at the fence. They watched the buybacks get tagged, and each one picked out their favorite Surfer Dude foal.

"On Thursday morning we prepared to go to the carnival grounds for the auction. The kids were excited to see which pony would be our first buyback [with the Chincoteague Legacy Group]. Got Milk's filly came into the ring. The bidding started and within minutes we won our buyback [with the Legacy Group]. We were all allowed into the ring to get a picture taken with the foal and each of the grandkids was able to pet the foal. It was an exciting time. A magical moment. Little did I know my life was about to change!"

After the excitement of the buyback, Darlene and her family returned to their seats to watch the rest of the auction.

"They asked if they could bid on a pony. I told Nicolette that she would have to ask her Pop Pop. After he said yes, I told her it would have to be a fall pickup to give us time to prepare for a foal and I gave her a spending limit. I wanted her to be prepared if the bidding went too high."

©2015 Melissa Hottenstein

Darlene said the kids were on pins and needles, watching as each new foal came into the ring, and listening for the auctioneer to say if it was a fall pickup. When a tiny chestnut filly came into the ring, the auctioneer announced that this one would be a fall pickup.

"The kids were ready to start bidding, however, the auctioneer continued speaking," Darlene recalled.

"'This foal is special,' they said. She was brought in during the northern round up on the back of horse. She had a small leg wound. While taking care of her, the cowboys had to give her liquids. All they had was sweet tea and the filly loved it, so they have nicknamed her Sticky Sweet Tea.' The auctioneer informed us that the winner would also receive an autographed picture of her coming into the corral. The kids had already decided they wanted to bid on her. She was only a few weeks old and was tiny."

Darlene said Nicolette's hand shot into the air for the first bid.

"The bid spotter for our section asked us if she was bidding. We said yes, and the fun began. Someone else was bidding against us. We figured a fall pickup would go high. The bidding slowly went up and when it hit $750, I heard the auctioneer say SOLD!"

"We won a pony. I won a pony. What were we thinking? Everything happened so quickly!" Darlene said.

The spotter let them come into the ring to hug the filly and spend a few minutes with her, and to also get some photos.

"When we went over the booth to pay for our new filly it started sinking in that I had actually bought a Chincoteague Pony," Darlene said. "We came to the auction to be part of the CLG buyback. We had no intention of buying a pony!"

©2015 Melissa Hottenstein

But the grandkids were beyond excited. After the auction, they visited the foal and Nicolette, Isabella and Christopher discussed what to name her.

"We talked about the nickname the cowboys had given her and why they gave her that nickname. I asked them if we should keep it as her name. They all loved the idea of calling her Sweet Tea."

Darlene said, after researching Sweet Tea's pedigree she discovered how the name was even more fitting than they had imaged. Sweet Tea's granddam is Merry **Tea**Pot and her mother was **Sweet** Mischief.

"Sweet Tea seemed the right name for this little filly," she said.

Darlene laughs when she recalls the thoughts that raced through her head when she thought about taking the foal home. *Home? We didn't have a farm. We didn't have land for a pony. We would need to board her but where?*

It wasn't long until someone suggested she call Debbie Ober of the Chincoteague Pony Rescue and they arranged to board her there while they took the time they needed to learn more about caring for a Chincoteague Pony.

©2015 Melissa Hottenstein

"Over the next three months we got to watch her grow at the carnival grounds. She was a Momma's girl and rarely left her mother's side," Darlene said. "We were coming to the island to visit her and spend time getting to know her. We also visited Deb at the Chincoteague Pony Rescue and started learning about caring for our new filly [after she went there]. Our pony adventure had begun. We were trying to learn as much as we could."

The family visited the island again at Fall Roundup in October, watching Debbie load her onto the trailer for the trip to Ridgely, Maryland.

"She was not a happy camper. She did not want to be separated from her mother. She whinnied and stomped around the trailer. She let us know she didn't want to leave," Darlene said.

Darlene said she is grateful for the care Deb gave Sweet Tea, especially during that first year, helping her grow to become a healthy mare. They were able to visit time and time again, to bond and learn more.

In October of 2018, Sweet Tea - and a second Chincoteague Pony mare that the family adopted from the rescue – arrived home to a farm the family purchased in Florida.

©2020 Melissa Hottenstein

"Life is a series of adventures," Darlene said. "You never know where one moment will lead but if you are willing to step out in faith, amazing things can happen!"

Steven's Dream Dancer

Sometimes good intentions can go awry. That's we have to roll up our sleeves and go to work to make it all right.

Cindy Inserra came to the 2019 Pony Penning Auction with hope in her heart. She wanted to purchase a buyback foal as a way of honoring her late husband Steven.

"My husband and I had dreams, plans for our life as we got older," Cindy said. "Along the way it was always on my bucket list to someday go to Chincoteague. [When] I was a little girl I fell in love with "Misty of Chincoteague." After an abrupt shift in our lives, my husband had a short illness that took his young life too early. He died in February 2019, but before he died, we had a beautiful special time to be able to say things to each other that some people don't have a chance to do."

Cindy said, her husband Steven made her promise to live her life to its fullest and fulfill all her dreams, even if he could not be with her through it all.

"Traveling to Chincoteague just felt like a natural thing to do," she said. "So, I planned a trip with a friend of mine who is like a sister to me. Sharon and I drove from Syracuse to Chincoteague, excited about our trip."

On the long drive, Cindy said she jotted down names - for the buyback pony she planned to buy, one that she could visit in the wild annually.

Cindy said she and Sharon took their time becoming acclimated, following all the events that are attached to Pony Penning week. She stumbled upon The Feather Fund and then CLG - Chincoteague Legacy Group, making donations to both.

"Along the way we met many wonderful people," she said. "Somewhere in that mix, we were in the company of Keli and Grace Drew, but we never actually met."

Like   Comment

Tipson Myers and 205 others

Keli Drew
Love this baby. **Grace Drew** we better be saving for her!!!
36w   Like   Reply

Keli and her daughter Grace had been coming to Pony Penning for many years. This was the year they had planned to buy a foal, and they knew which one. On June 5, when Darcy Cole of DSC Photography posted a picture of Shy Anne and her beautiful new bay filly, they fell in love. Mom posted to daughter that this was the one they should buy. Then, on July 8, their beloved horse Toffee slipped and fell in the pasture.

"We had to have him put down and that used our baby - and vacation - money," Keli said. "We had to shorten our trip to Chincoteague."

While acclimating to the island, Cindy learned that the price for a buyback pony was well beyond her budget.

"So, I thought of a plan B," Cindy said, "to look for someone that I thought might deserve a pony. I wanted to pay it forward to that person and buy them a pony."

The evening before Pony Penning, Cindy said she and Sharon went to the pens to see the ponies.

"We stood up against the fence, just mesmerized looking at these gorgeous ponies," she said. "I asked Sharon, how do they know what ponies get auctioned and who decides what pony goes where? As Sharon and I were wondering, the woman standing next to us answered my question with much knowledge."

Cindy said the woman introduced herself as "Jean".

"She was holding a book that had every pony's picture in it and every statistic about every pony in it. We felt she was a seasoned pony penning person with a lot of knowledge. We talked for a bit and learned that she was hoping to buy a pony but had fallen on hard times and now couldn't afford to buy a pony. She went on to tell us that she had a stall all ready for a pony and a family back home ready to welcome a new pony."

Cindy's heart was pounding. Maybe this was the person she was looking for. She began to ask more questions. She said it almost felt like an interview.

"I asked her several key questions on taking care of a pony," she said. "I have horses at home, so I knew what owning a horse entails. I wanted to see if perhaps she was the one I should buy a pony for."

Auction day came early. The sun was just up when they met Jean inside the auction ring. They took a seat and waited for the right pony. Foal # 15 came into the arena. The auctioneer asked, "Do we have a little buckskin here?" That seemed to interest Jean. But then, when the filly

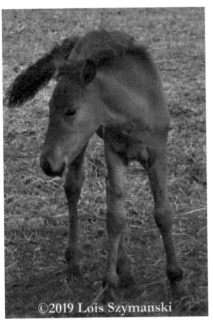

©2019 Lois Szymanski

came into the middle of the ring, he quickly noted that this was a bay filly. Jean turned to them and said this was the one.

"I won the auction for pony number 15," Cindy said. "I went up to the podium with Jean to purchase our winning pony. When the auction lady asked me for information I pointed to Jean and said, 'I just want to pay for the pony.' I walked away and left Jean to do the rest. It was my idea to remain anonymous… to just pay it forward."

But Cindy said something did not feel right.

"When we left, Sharon and I both had a pit in our stomachs. I just had a bad feeling. It didn't feel like I thought it would feel "giving back".

As they walked to the pens to find the foal. Jean started to throw a fit, insisting the fire company had switched foals. She believed they had purchased a buckskin, not a bay. People around them said the woman was babbling, making no sense at all, and soon it became clear that she had no knowledge of horses, no property to keep one on, and no money to support a horse.

"As luck would have it, we met a woman there who was at the [CLG] bonfire that Keli and Grace were at too. Her name is Wendy. After the commotion of Jean complaining she got the wrong pony, it was Wendy who told us that there was a mother and daughter who really wanted that pony. They'd even given their phone number to Jean. She would try to find them."

Cindy said she knew she had to get the papers away from Jean, to take that foal back.

As she walked away, Cindy was beside herself. What was meant to be a good deed was not turning out so well after all.

"We had planned on leaving the next morning for home, but I wasn't leaving the island until I knew that pony's fate," Cindy said.

Cindy's determination was the start of something good. Sometimes, in life, a circle of protection comes along and there is a balancing of sorts, a power to right all wrongs.

That evening, they ran into Jean again at the carnival grounds. Cindy spoke up, asking her to give the foal up. A small group of folks gathered around, including Wendy. They all realized the foal needed them.

Wendy Hoatson was determined to save this foal. She went to the announcement booth to look for a fire company representative, who joined them all in trying to talk sense into Jean, but she gripped the foal papers tighter, more determined than ever. Along came an off duty Chincoteague policeman, who was also a saltwater cowboy, a man who knew horses. He soon realized that this woman was not capable of taking care of a foal. Calmly, choosing his words with care, the policeman worked to convince Jean that she was in over her head. It was literally midnight on Thursday night when she finally gave up the papers for the baby.

"Although I felt embarrassed about my poor judgement, I went on to own my mistake and make it right for the sake of the pony," Cindy said.

Inside the bag with the paperwork Jean had finally relinquished, Cindy found a torn piece from a Krispy Cream box. There was a phone number on it.

"Wendy told me then that she thought that was the phone number of the people who were desperately trying to talk Jean into giving up the pony the day before, at the pens," Cindy said. "By now it was too late to call that number, so everyone went their own way and we went back to our hotel. I went to bed wondering [about] this pony's fate. I wondered if I was going home with her or if I could find this mystery mother and daughter in time before we had to leave."

At 7 a.m. the next morning, Cindy picked up the phone and called the mysterious number.

"Lo and behold, it was Grace," she said. "Instantly there was a connection and that fear in the pit of my stomach was gone! I knew I had the right people. We planned to meet at the pen at 10 a.m. and it was then that I felt a great divine intervention had taken place."

©2019 Keli & Grace Drew

As she watched them load the foal to go home, Cindy realized that – even though the journey had been a rollercoaster ride – things were now right with the world.

"After crying happy tears over our incredible story, Grace mentioned that she was hoping to have the word Dreamer in [the filly's] name. I was shocked, because most of the names I had jotted down had the word

Dreamer in them! I told her I had some names on my phone but since she wasn't a buyback, I didn't think it was up to me what her name should be. It was up to Grace. She immediately wanted to hear those names, and to my delight she chose Steven's Dream Dancer."

"Grace asked me who Steven was," and that's when Cindy told her about her husband and how she had lost him just five months earlier.

"I know my husband is a very strong spirit and it was his divine intervention - along with the help of angels and Jesus - that this was meant to be," Cindy said. "I cannot describe that feeling of pure love. I will never forget my story and I thank Steven every day for Stevie and all of the people involved. Every single person had an important

©2020
Keli & Grace Drew

Keli says Stevie's kindness shows in her gentle eyes.

role in finding Grace and Keli. I believe it was supposed to happen this way and I am forever grateful."

Grace agreed.

"Everything that happened around Stevie and leading up to us getting her was just meant to be," she said. "That's the only baby I wanted to bring home."

Steven's Dream Dancer has a bright new future with this mother daughter team in her new home in Pennsylvania.

"Stevie is our dream come true, miracle pony that mended broken hearts and she blesses us every day," Grace said.

Her mom agreed.

"I don't know how to describe what it means to have Stevie," Keli said. "She's a real blessing, and she really was meant to be ours. She's a reminder to live life to the fullest too and cherish every moment we have with our loved ones."

On one of her visits, Cindy got to hug the foal whose life she saved. In the future, Grace and Keli plan to train Stevie for trail and pleasure riding, but mostly, they plan to love her. Sometimes, with faith, perseverance, and a lot of luck, things work out the way they are supposed to.

Cindy visits Steven's Dream Dancer "Stevie" in her new Pennsylvania home.

PFFs – Pony Friends Forever

The connection between those who love and follow the Chincoteague Ponies is not easy to explain. A thread runs through this community, connecting pony-lovers at random, drawing us together and making us care about one another. Like the sticky threads of a spiderweb, sometimes they pull us together when we least expect it. That's what happened when Sue Johnstonbaugh met the Price family.

On her drive to Chincoteague for Pony Penning 2018, Sue said she was thinking about the roundup, meeting up with friends, photographing the foals, all the things that are a part of the best week of every year. That's when she saw the pickup truck carrying two colorful kayaks that was following her south on Route 113 in Maryland. The traffic had slowed, with an obvious jam up ahead. Sue's mom has a house on the island, so she knew a shortcut. She turned right to detour.

Steve Price was riding his brakes on and off, a necessity with the traffic mess ahead. When the silver car in front of him with the Chincoteague bumper stickers turned right, he decided to follow.

"I bet she knows a shortcut," he told his wife Kathy. In the back seat, Kathy and Steve's teen twins, Carl and John listened in.

Sue said she noticed the truck had followed her and she started to wonder if they were going to Chincoteague, too.

"They continued to follow me down Route 13, through Maryland and into Virginia and they passed me a few times on the way. When they passed me, a young man in the back seat of the pickup truck held up pictures of Chincoteague Ponies in a binder."

Sue said, her special license plates and many stickers of Chincoteague on the back window were a sure give away. She knew at once that they were headed to Pony Penning.

"When we got to T's Corner and turned left, I motioned out of my window for the pickup truck to pull over behind me. We pulled over into the grassy area where the fruit stand normally is. I jumped out of my car and headed toward the pickup truck as they all got out."

Sue said she asked, 'Are you heading to Chincoteague?' That's when Steve stepped forward and introduced himself and his family. "John is a Feather Fund recipient this year," he said.

Sue said she couldn't help but smile. She'd already heard about John and the essay he'd written for the Feather Fund in a conversation with me, so she knew this was a great family.

"I was so excited to meet this young man," she said. "I felt like I was meeting a celebrity! We talked about his essay and I told him how good I was told it was and he offered for me to read it right there in the grassy area where we had pulled off, on the side of Chincoteague Road."

As she finished reading the essay, Sue said Kathy told John to, "Show her your binder."

"The 3-ring binder had his favorite Chincoteague foals in it," Sue said. "He has great taste in foals and ponies, and I loved every one. I remember secretly hoping he would get Got Milk's [colt], but I know that her foals always sell for a lot of money."

Sue is the kind of person who is always sharing with others. She had some decals with her that had feathers on them with the word "Dream" and she ran to her trunk to find one to give to John.

"I had planned to give [both] Feather Fund kids a decal when I met them," she said. "After chatting for a few more minutes, we parted ways and they followed me to Chincoteague, over the causeway. I reminded them they had to roll their windows down on the way over the causeway to smell the marsh air. It's a tradition many of us follow."

Throughout the week, the two saw each other many times at the pony pens. Sue said she had her eyes on the Feather Fund kids at auction, rooting for each of them to win their favorite foals. When John won the bid on Got Milk's foal, she said it made her cry happy tears.

©2018 Kathy Price

"Traveling to the island that day, we knew it would be a memorable trip with new friendships. But we couldn't have imagined..." John's mom, Kathy Price said. "When we pulled over at T's corner, I thought for a second... what are we doing... pulling over to meet some stranger along a road we aren't familiar with. Is this really a smart decision?"

But Kathy said she knows now that it was a great decision.

"Sue was sent to escort us to the island," she said. "She is the best welcoming committee. Her gift to John that day represents her big heart and the inspiration of all of our PFFs [Pony Friends Forever]. The way she enthusiastically introduced herself and welcomed our family was the perfect beginning to a week we will never forget."

Kathy said Sue helped make John feel important on that day, and she continues to do the same every time they meet, online or in person.

John named his new colt Bandit. At home, he quickly bonded with the colt and training and desensitization began. As the bond deepened, Sue kept in touch.

Since their chance roadside meeting, Sue has become good friends with the family. She's traveled to Pennsylvania to visit them and even to watch John compete in an IEA (Interscholastic Equestrian Association) Western competition where he rode the horse that was assigned to him.

©2019 Kathy Price

John is getting Bandit out into the world. He visited a Tractor Supply Store as a foal at Christmastime and has already taken the colt to several shows. He was even a part of the Chincoteague Pony Breed demonstrations held at the Horse World Expo in 2019 and 2020. Sue made sure she was there for both Expos, to cheer for John and Bandit.

"Sue is an amazing friend," John said. "She supports me in all my activities. It meant the world to me when she came to watch me compete in my horse show."

John & Bandit at the 2020 Horse World Expo

©2020 Lois Szymanski

"He even got a ribbon!" Sue said excitedly. "I speak to both Steve and Kathy online and I've been to their house and farm a few times. We've given each other gifts, too - but having met them the way I did makes it that much better!"

"Steve and Kathy, John and [his twin brother] Carl and their grandmother, Phyllis are very special to me," Sue said. "And so are Bandit, Sam and Jax [the family horses]. I'm so happy to have met this family," she said. "Chincoteague is the magical island that united us."

John agrees that this unexpected bond is one to cherish, as is his relationship with his beautiful gelding, Bandit.

Bandit is my best friend," John said. "He always knows how to make me smile. He amazes me, and it means the world to me to be with him every day. I plan on showing him at the Horse World Expo and other shows. My future plan is to train him to be an all-around pony, so we can ride Western and English, along with going on trail rides."

Photo courtesy of Sue Johnstonbaugh

When Wildest Dreams Come True

Kathy O'Dette says she cannot remember a time when she did not love horses, from childhood up. She said her dad was a sweet man who took every opportunity to fulfill her horse obsession, despite his uneasiness around them. Here is her story, exactly as she sent it to me.

"There were endless pony rides and riding stable horse rentals that he chauffeured me to, waiting patiently until I was done," she said. "I was an only child, and the three of us started attending local horse shows within an hour or so from our small Northeastern Connecticut town. We all enjoyed it, but I longed for a pony of my own of course. My parents were textile factory workers, and although we had our own house and the necessities, there would never be enough extra money for a pony.

Fast forward and it is 1983. My best friend tells me that she is going to Chincoteague, Virginia with her friend who is a writing an article about Pony Penning for her hometown newspaper in Rhode Island. My very first thought was "Misty – that's where the wild ponies are!" I told [my husband] Michael about the book I had loved as a child, and, out of the blue, he said, 'Let's go too'.

So, we drove from Connecticut to Chincoteague in July of 1983. From then on until this day, I [felt as if I] was on the most magical journey of my life. We loved the island of Chincoteague and experienced our first pony swim. As first timers, we arrived at the pony auction toward the end – standing room only. When it was over, Michael announced "I'll go home and build a barn, and next year we'll come back and buy one". I listened in disbelief!

We returned to Connecticut and he started barn construction. The aircraft and auto mechanic who enjoyed speed and riding motorcycles, was now as caught up in buying a Chincoteague foal as I was. I spent the months until July 1984 reading a book called "How to Raise and Train a Foal". What I lacked in hands on horse experience in my 33 years, I made up for in devouring every bit of information on horses and their behavior.

We arrived in Chincoteague at the start of the week and were at the corral Monday morning to see the Northern Herd being driven into the Southern corral on Assateague. I loved every foal and every pony I saw, but I wanted a pinto more than anything. When we returned to the corral later that afternoon, the saltwater cowboys were still trying to round up the last band of Southern ponies. That year, a news crew was filming for a show called *PM Magazine*. They filmed this elusive band led by a black and white boss mare. I learned years later that the firemen had named her "Mappy". The herd's stallion was small, a solid red color. Together the mare and stallion were quite the team, but they were finally penned with the rest of the ponies.

Thursday, July 26, 1984 was auction day! The first five foals went quickly. Then, enter #6, a small pinto, introduced by Bernie [Pleasants] the auctioneer as "taking after his daddy" with regard to sex. My only memory from that point on was "sold for $250". I was both ecstatic and in shock. I owned a Chincoteague Pony!!

After purchasing a tiny blue halter, we made our way to the holding pen for the newly purchased foals. "What number?" asked fireman, David Savage, whom we recognized from our conversations throughout that week. He was very

© Kathy O'Dette

knowledgeable about the ponies and seemed to be so patient with spectators, many of whom asked the same questions over and over. When I proudly responded, 'Number six', his immediate reply was "Oh, the kicker". *Oh my, what had I gotten myself into*, I wondered?

We arranged for Stormy's transport to Connecticut and after watching the return of the remaining ponies to Assateague on Friday, we headed for home to put the finishing touches on his little barn. I waited for his arrival for what seemed like an eternity (but in reality, only a week). When he was led off the trailer, he looked even smaller than what I remembered. I led him into the barn, and he promptly kicked me in the stomach. *Oh my, what had I really gotten myself into?*

PM Magazine aired their story on the pony swim and auction. Watching it brought back all the excitement of that Monday when I watched the cowboys pen that last southern band of ponies. But wait – who is the foal that is running alongside the black and white mare – it sure looks like my Stormy! After rewinding the recording several times, I discovered it was

© Kathy O'Dette

indeed my Stormy. I now knew who his dam and probable sire were – Mappy, who was the boss mare of the band, and that little red stallion who was so very feisty!

My Stormy was the absolute perfect pony. The trainer called him Stormy the Wonder Pony, because, as she said, 'He's a wonderful pony!' The first time I sat on his back I felt completely safe and at ease. By then I had been taking dressage lessons, and I had bought a full size horse to ride in the meantime. Apollo was a beautiful Palomino, but he turned out to be a "bolter". As a beginner adult rider, any confidence I had gained was pretty much shattered. Stormy restored it on that very first ride – he was worth his weight in gold to me. We competed in some small dressage shows. I was extremely nervous, but he was not. He impressed some of the most well-known and toughest dressage judges on the East Coast.

We learned that "horses are herd animals", and so it came to pass that we would purchase another Chincoteague foal, hopefully from the same band as Stormy. In July of 1985 we were headed to Chincoteague again, with a newly purchased horse trailer in tow. We arrived Sunday afternoon and after hastily setting up camp at Maddox Family Campground, we drove to Assateague to get our first look at the ponies. We kept our eyes open for Mappy and the little red stallion. We were soon rewarded when we spotted the whole band grazing in a clearing on Assateague. That's when we spotted a flashy looking red and white pinto colt in the herd.

In the days following we spent hours at the southern corral watching the flashy pinto and the other foals, including that adorable little pinto filly. Which one would we bid on? It was decided that we would bid on whichever one came up first.

On July 25, 1985, we were excited to purchase a companion for Stormy. The bidding started. Foal after foal was auctioned, and still no sign of either of the two that we had so diligently studied that week. Finally, number 24 was up for sale, and it was the flashy red and white colt! As luck would have it, another bidder wanted him also, and the bidding went back and forth between the two of us. After what seemed like forever, we were "all in all done" with our bid of $500. I named him Chief because for some reason he reminded me of a little Indian pony, and his red color reminded me of fire, and after all, this was all about raising money for the Chincoteague Fire Department, right? So Chief it was.

We trailered Chief back to Connecticut, along with a cute palomino foal which we dropped off in Southern Connecticut for his owners. At the time, Stormy was at a trainer to start his basic long line work. I wanted to spend time with Chief alone and win his trust, but that took a lot longer than with Stormy.

I always felt that Chief was so much closer to "wild". He was tough in body and spirit, and bold as brass. He so reminded me of his probable sire – the little red stallion who we'd witnessed

© Kathy O'Dette

challenging the bigger stallions and protecting his mares when all the bands were together in the corrals.

There were several different postcards over the years which featured this band, who were part of the Southern Herd and easily accessible. We felt even more a part of history whenever we discovered new photos of them in the little shops on the island.

Provided Courtesy of Kathy O'Dette

GREETINGS FROM
Chincoteague Island, Virginia

As we had hoped, Stormy and Chief became buddies. I spent many happy hours riding Stormy while my friend rode Chief. Chief was a bit too fast for me, but he had a partner in my friend Nancy. Chief and Nancy would blaze the trail while Stormy and I followed. Chief was always first, but he would wait for Stormy and I to catch up, all the while reaching behind to undo the velcro on Nancy's sneakers! That was Chief. With that red coloring he reminded me of the pony version of Dennis the Menace. Chief was always *the helper*, although his help around the barn with tools, rakes, hammers and the like was not always appreciated.

Stormy and Chief were inseparable in so many ways for 25 years. When Stormy suddenly developed a neurological condition, which would necessitate me making the decision to end his suffering within an hour, my heart was broken. On top of that, I so feared that soon after I would lose Chief also. But to my relief, he did fine as my remaining Chincoteague.

© Kathy O'Dette

I believe Chief knew that he had an obligation to me to stick around at least a few more years. I never dreamed he would move across the country with me for the second time at 29 years of age - from New Mexico to North Carolina. I always knew that Stormy was my "heart pony", but after this move, I came to realize that Chief was too – just in a different way.

This downsizing in my life resulted in having to find the perfect boarding situation. After having my ponies and horses in my own back yard, it was hard to trust anyone to care for Chief the way I had. Yet sometimes things just work out. We both became members of the best small dressage barn family. Windcroft Farm's owner, Becky Blikslager had a soft spot for ponies, and took amazing care of her new charges.

I groomed, visited, walked and strengthened my bond with Chief over the next four years. I realized that just being with him brought me such joy. I didn't even have to ride to experience it. My little wild pony became the barn's pony mascot and babysitter for any nervous newcomer to the barn. He taught many who never would have met a real Chincoteague about the hardy, trustworthy, kindhearted Chincoteague breed. Now that they are both gone, I believe Stormy and Chief are back on the island of Assateague. They will live on in my heart forever. They were a dream-come-true in so many ways," Kathy said.

While I was working on the book, and as we corresponded, Kathy shared another amazing fact. On a trip to Florida, who do you think she found?

Kathy meets Mappy in Florida

It was Mappy, dam of her first Chinco-teague Pony, Stormy. The mare had been removed from the island and relocated to live in Florida with Stan White. How excited she was to be able to visit with the beautiful mare who had given her the foal who made her dream-come-true. Talk about things coming full circle.

With Facebook, Kathy has been able to connect with so many others who love the breed the way she does.

"My Chincoteague experiences have culminated in a unique bond that I feel with all other Chincoteague owners and lovers of the breed," Kathy said. "There is a nostalgia about those old ponies whose lineage may not have been known back then, but who live on forever in the ponies that now live on Assateague. My story may seem quite ordinary to many, but for me it is the best story ever – beyond my wildest dreams.

©Kathy O'Dette

Checkers & Her Curly Fry

Born in 1997, the mare Checkers has had a checkered past, no pun intended. She's moved from herd to herd over the years and at some point, her eye was injured, resulting in it being removed, but this resilient mare has a way of always bouncing back. She proved this again, not long ago, in 2017 when she sustained a leg injury, one that would sideline any other mare.

Saltwater Cowboy, Hunter Leonard shared how, after getting a call from someone who saw Checker's limping, the cowboys rounded her up for a vet check.

©2014 Lois Szymanski

"It turns out, she had cut the suspension tendon, located right here," he said, indicating the area just under the fetlock. "Every time she walked her leg went straight to the ground. It looked awful. It looked super painful."

Hunter said they were not sure if the tendon would repair itself, but they cared for the mare inside the Leonard barn for several months, trying multiple methods to get it to heal.

"It finally got to the point where we had to take her back [to her herd on Assateague] to see if she could make it. You have to give them a shot," he said. "If she couldn't keep up, we would know really quick."

She not only made it, she had a foal a few months later, in September. To insure they would do okay, the mare and foal were brought to the Leonard Farm.

"We didn't even know she was pregnant," Hunter said. "That foal came out with the curliest hair. He had the biggest curls for a foal."

Courtesy Sydney Murdock

Hunter said Checkers (who some call Giraffe) will always have this injury. She seems to take it in stride, but if you watch her closely you can still see that her fetlock drops lower on that leg whenever she walks.

"When she takes off running you can see that she can run just fine," Hunter said. And she continues to do well in the wild.

That fall, Sydney Murdock, who was visiting the island from California, bought the foal. All those curls made her smile. She named her new colt

Curley Fry Extra Salty.

"I was lucky enough to go with one of my friends, Chelsie Kenlon, to the Leonard Farm," Sydney said. "When I was there, I saw this sweet little foal with two others. The other two had brands. But he didn't. He was the fluffiest cutest little thing. I asked what was going on with him and they said the fire company hadn't

©2017 Sydney Murdock

company hadn't decided yet. We asked if they would sell him to us."

Sydney said they were surprised when they heard their offer was accepted. Then they had to scramble to figure out how to get him home, all the way to San Diego, California.

Soon enough, the new colt arrived in California, moving onto their Rancho Costalotta. But it wasn't long until this traveling foal was back on the road again. The Murdock family had decided their hearts were on Chincoteague Island. They found a lovely farm located just off the island on the mainland, purchased it, and the Murdocks moved east.

Curley Fry has a happy life with the family at their Rancho Costalotta East, sharing the farm with a miniature donkey, a miniature pony, multiple horses, rabbits, chickens, ducks and geese. It's a happy menagerie with lots of love – a place where Curly Fry fits right in.

©2018 Sydney Murdock

"Curly fry is such a character. He has so much personality," Sydney said. "I swear he knows and understands what I am saying to him. He isn't afraid of anything and is always up for whatever I come up with. He is incredibly smart - and almost too smart at that. But he keeps me on my toes."

Sydney's mom, Colleen Murdock agrees. "I think he's pretty awesome. Such an even temperament. He can go long periods with no work and then go right back to it like he does it daily. The voice commands Sydney taught him impress me every time."

©2019 Sydney Murdock

"I'm incredibly happy we ended up in each other's lives," Sydney said. "I plan to do anything and everything with him. From liberty and tricks, to pony hunter/ jumper shows!"

Norm – A Stud with a Story

Sometimes the story of how a pony becomes a permanent herd member on the Chincoteague Wildlife Refuge is a testament to that old saying, "It was meant to be." That is the case with young Norman Rockwell Giddings, a stud with a story.

It all started with the beautiful mare, Babe, who spent a lifetime on

© 2019 Lois Szymanski

Assateague Island, the buyback of the Giddings family.

Casie Giddings tells the story of her dad, one of five kids - "born smack dab in the middle," she said. "His father (Casie's grandfather) Norman was blind, so they seldom took vacations, but one year, they did, going to Chincoteague Island in 1968."

Casie said that vacation must have been a memorable one for her dad, because he took his own young family there in 1994, surprising them by purchasing a buyback filly for a whopping $850. That mare was named

Babe. Over the years, the selection of foals who would remain on the island never seemed to include Babe's foals, something that Darcy Cole took note of.

Anyone who follows the Chincoteague Ponies knows Darcy, a regular hiker who walks miles and miles to document the ponies. She keeps us all in the loop, recording which stallion each mare is with, accounting for breedings, photographing and documenting new foal births and sharing photos on the DSC Photography page daily.

Darcy remembers telling the Giddings family that she hoped Babe's next foal would be a buyback, to keep that line going. She thought the foal would be by Legacy after she witnessed them breeding on January 1st of 2017, but when that breeding didn't take, a later one with Puzzle did, producing a beautifully marked bay pinto colt.

"We were very disappointed that he wasn't picked as a buyback," Darcy said of the 2018 colt, "but then the person that got him [Cherie Miner] decided to keep him a stallion and we were thrilled that his bloodlines would still be carried on."

©2018 DSC Photography

Casie said she made it a point to talk to Cherie after the auction.

"After the auction, I'd talked to Cherie and told her how much we loved him and [how I] had hoped he'd be chosen as a buyback and that he was extra special because not only was he likely Babe's last foal, but also that he was born on my grandfather's birthday," Casie said.

Casie's grandfather Norman and his wife – her grandmother – had both passed within three months of each other in 2015, leaving a hole in the family.

"Cherie asked me what my grandfather's name was and I didn't think much of it, until her Facebook post late that same night, where she graciously chose to include my grandfather in the naming of her pony. What she didn't know, is that my other Grandmom (my mom's mom that had passed on in 2005) was named Norma after her father, so the name has even more meaning to us."

Cherie's post on July 27, 2018 read, "Hello everyone! I am the owner of foals #30 and #50, Susana's and Babe's colts respectively. They are being trailered by the wonderful Jenna Kay Jordan and Jaylee Jordan and we will hopefully be going to pick them up very soon. We purchased our first three Chincoteague fillies in 2014, trained and sold two of them, and I am currently working (very slowly) at putting my Marshy under saddle."

Cherie wrote, "I wanted to share the names we picked for our boys. I always put LOTS of thought into names. It's my favorite part! For our ponies I like to name them something that combines the meanings of the [names of the] dam and sire. #50 is out of Babe and Puzzle. This is a special name that ties in many meanings… First, this is the name of my favorite American painter. He has painted many scenes of American life and plenty of artwork containing people playing cards and board games [and that] ties in with his sire's name Puzzle… And lastly, we learned from one of Babe's buy back owners, Casie Leigh, that this special colt was born on what would have been her grandfather, Norman's birthday."

Casie said her heart was filled with joy when she read the post.

"So I introduce to you all to Norman Rockwell (Norm)," Cherie wrote. "He is very special to us and Lord willing, will remain a stud for future beautiful Chincoteague babies."

Cherie had amazing plans. Norman's first year was spent with her small herd of Chincoteague ponies, but, as life is sometimes more hectic than we plan, Cherie came to realize she didn't have the time she'd hoped for to train and work with Norm. He was a young stud who needed a lot of attention. With some trepidation, she put the word out that she needed to find a good home for Norm.

When I saw the post that he was for sale," Darcy said, "I contacted the Chincoteague Volunteer Fire Company and asked them - if we bought him if they would accept him back to the herd as a donation? I knew it was a long shot, but I had to at least try."

Darcy said when she got word that the fire company would take him and that they agreed his bloodlines would be good for the herd she was excited beyond description.

Casie said Darcy called her to share the news.

"I was just getting ready to leave work and of course, it was emotional," she said.

But then something else happened. Right after her grandfather had passed, Casie's family started seeing praying mantis' frequently, in random places. And on this day, right after she got the news and was leaving the office, Casie saw a praying mantis.

"I knew everything was going to work out," she said. And it did.

©2020 Debbie Ehst

With the help of a small group of donors organized by Darcy, Norman was purchased. Her post announcing the news was a giant thank you to the donors, to Tipson Myers for donating her time and hauling services, for visiting the farm ahead of time and for keeping Norm at her farm for a short time. She thanked veterinarian, Allison Dotzel for donating an examination, vaccinations, and worming, and she included a big thank you to Chincoteague Volunteer Fire Company for agreeing to accept this donation back to the herd. With a boatload of support, Norm came home to Chincoteague in October of 2019.

"It was in honor of that grandfather in Babe's buy back family who instilled the love of Chincoteague in his children and grandchildren, that we added Giddings to his name, [making his] full name Norman Rockwell Giddings, with a call name of Norm," Darcy said. "Not keeping him last year was the right thing to do for Babe. I don't think she would have made it through the summer if she had nursed him until Fall Roundup."

Casie echoed the same thoughts, adding, "Our precious Norm has such a wonderful story. It is a miracle how everything came together. It truly took a circle of love to make it happen. Never in our wildest pony dreams

©2020 Debbie Ehst

did we think we had a chance of him ever returning after he wasn't chosen as a buyback in 2018. We are eternally grateful to everyone who helped make our dream a reality, and for whom we share sponsorship of Norm with. It truly takes a village."

Darcy agreed.

"The outpouring of love and how so many people came together to allow for Norm to make his way back home, still gets me choked up," Casie said. "We knew it was a long shot. I'm not sure of everything that went on behind the scenes to make it happen between Darcy, the CVFD, and countless others, but we couldn't have done it without each and every one of them! I'm a firm believer in that everything happens for a reason and by the grace of God everything worked out beautifully!"

Prince Snipperdoodle

The sheer determination and drive so many have to make their Chincoteague Pony dream come true never ceases to amaze me. We hear about the girl who raised money at a lemonade stand, the one who got chickens and sold eggs, the kids who save all their birthday and Christmas money... And then there's Julie Childs – who made and sold $1100 worth of ponchos to save for her pony.

At the age of 11, Julie read the book "Misty of Chincoteague" and – like so many – fell in love with Chincoteague Ponies.

"After I was done reading it, I was curious if the ponies were real and if they still had the auction," Julie said.

After researching online, Julie decided she had to have her own Chincoteague Pony. That's when she learned how to make polar fleece ponchos, selling them and saving every penny earned. She said her Aunt Laura taught her how to make them, and together, they spread the word, setting up at craft shows and tack sales to sell.

"People would tell their friends about my project," Julie said. "I also went to different craft shows and tack sales to spread the word about my venture. I had a paper route and I did other jobs to raise money to be able to bid on a pony at the 2005 auction."

Julie and her mom planned the trip, inviting friends to join them on their adventure of a lifetime.

"We got the trailer ready with a water tub and the truck and we packed the van to the seams," she said.

Julie said the saltwater cowboys already had ponies in the pens when they arrived. She could not wait to find her favorite foals.

"We saw stallions, mares, foals, yearlings," she said. "It was so exciting! I started to look at all of the ponies and foals. I had my heart set on a paint or a buckskin. But then, I ended up looking at a foal that was standing next to his dam and just chilling. Its coat was a light brown and had a gold tint on its tail and on its legs."

The next day, Julie and her crew slogged through marsh muck to see the swim. Julie said her shoe was sucked right off her foot.

"No one told us to get the best view of the swim, we would have to wade through black muck almost up to our knees!"

Finally, they found a spot to set up their chairs, a few rows back from the orange fencing. Just on the other side, the ponies would rest after swimming before being paraded through town.

"After a couple hours, we heard from the fire department that the Saltwater Cowboys were getting ready. [It was] slack tide, time to swim the horses across."

Back at the carnival grounds, Julie watched the foals race back and forth, playing tag with each other, doing zoomies around their dams.

"I double checked the ponies I was hoping to bid on. I saw the light brown one again. My mom said, 'Don't bid on that one. It's cow hocked and scrawny.' I looked at the other foals and wrote their numbers down on a list so I would be ready to bid the next day."

After leaving the pens, Julie's family and friends headed to Assateague for beach time. The waves were huge that day, perhaps a warning of what was to come.

"All of a sudden, Irma, mom's friend, fell and broke her leg. The ambulance came and took her to a hospital, but she was sent back to our camp that night with crutches, a cast and pain pills."

The next day was auction. As she watched horses of all colors, pintos, buckskins, chestnut and bay… come into the ring, Julie realized they were selling for a lot of money, more than she had raised. Her heart sank.

"I was becoming a bit disappointed. Then [a foal] was brought out that was going to need care on its eye. No one was bidding, so I decided to place a bid. I thought, *Maybe this is my pony.* I wanted to help it and love it. Then, all of a sudden, people around me started to bid and another person took that foal home."

Julie swallowed her anxiety. The auction was nearing its end.

"Every foal on my list or off of my list sold for more than the $1200 I had earned to buy my foal," she said. "They had a couple solid colored foals left to be auctioned. I was standing up when the fire department brought out a light brown foal with a snip as its only marking. My mom said to bid. So, I did, with the help of my friend, Cathy - who helped the spotter see my bids. I was

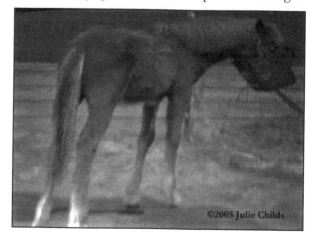

©2005 Julie Childs

very, very excited when the auctioneer said, "Sold to the girl in the orange poncho!'"

For $1100, Julie had her foal.

"When my mom looked at him, wouldn't you know, it was the foal she had told me not to buy!" Julie said.

The foal would not be alone on the long haul home. A friend in the group had also purchased a dark bay filly with two white socks.

© Julie Childs

"The next day, when we took our red stock trailer to the carnival grounds to pick the foals up, I looked at my foal and said, 'You cute little Snipperdoodle.' It was not one of the names on my list, but he became Prince Snipperdoodle."

Prince Snipperdoodle celebrated his 15th birthday in the spring of 2020. The 13.2 hand liver chestnut has done it all, but there were trials and tribulations along the way. At age two, he pulled away from her mom to run to Julie and broke her mom's arm. After that, he was gelded.

"When he was 10, he got his leg stuck in the fence and stood for hours. He was great at MSU Vet Clinic and did not even need sedation for the examination,," Julie said.

Then, there was the time he cantered under an apple tree, sweeping Julie from his back, and the time they were riding at Ionia State Recreation Park and she ended up in a rose bush when he slammed to a stop from a full gallop, sending her flying. What an adventure this life with Snipperdoodle has been.

"He also enjoyed going to visit the judges during riding classes," Julie shared with a laugh.

Despite the hiccoughs, Snipperdoodle has competed in so many disciplines, excelling at all. He's shown in Speed, English, Western, Saddle Seat, Halter, Showmanship, and dressage. They went to their State 4-H Horse Fair twice, even though, during one of those competitions, he jumped out of the dressage ring!

Photo Courtesy of Julie Childs

"He has always been quite whimsical and free thinking," Julie said. "The second time we qualified, I showed in western along with the other classes. He's gone to the Ohio Equine Affaire to be the demo pony for Gavin Robson - starting a green horse in driving. I also showed Snip in 2017 in dressage at a Kiwanis Show in Ohio. We placed first and I have a video of him taking the letter F during the test. It was later returned after I went past… the volunteer got confused!"

Photo Courtesy of Julie Childs

As a driving horse, Snip has been to the National Drive - both at the Kentucky Horse Park and the Hoosier Horse Park.

"We showed at the 2018 Metamora Combined Driving event in training level, and Snip placed 3rd at the North American Preliminary Driving Championship I 2019 at Metamora, Michigan.
There, he was awarded the Best Conditioned Pony at the whole event," Julie said.

Snip has been used at a Peggy Brown clinic as a driving pony and has participated with the Mid-Michigan Color Guard in parades.

Photo courtesy July Childs

Snipperdoodle – who is now a therapeutic driving pony – is proof that Chincoteague Ponies, even the free thinking ones - can do it all!

Julie said she often tells Prince Snipperdoodle, "Snip, you are smart, whimsical, opinionated, and cute and I am glad we ended up together no matter what my Mom said so many years ago!"

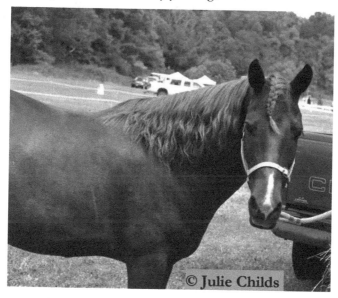

© Julie Childs

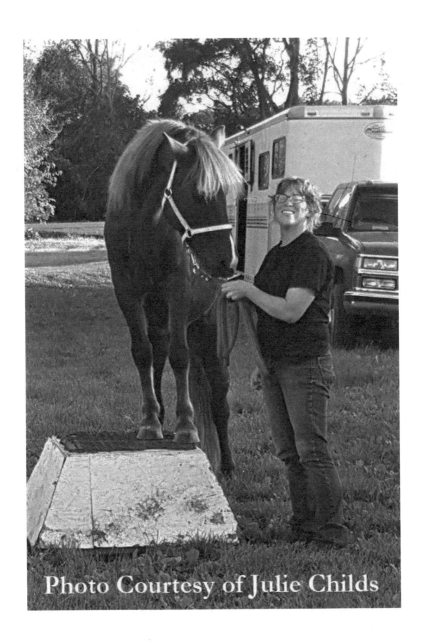

Photo Courtesy of Julie Childs

Orphan Tales

2007 brought a hot and muggy summer season. Day after day featured humidity so thick a person could sweat standing still. It was a day like this that Chincoteague's own Leonard family took friends from England on a pontoon cruise along the Assateague shoreline.

Saltwater cowboy, Hunter Leonard was 10 years old that year. He recalled the trip with his dad's friend, Dr. Morgan and his extended family – three generations, seven people.

"We sailed up in Cherry Tree Hill Bay where our clubhouse is. That's where we go duck hunting. As we rolled up, looking across the water, you could see a baby running around all alone. That's a bad area," Hunter said. "I would not ride my horse up there. The mud is as thick as it can get. If you stepped in, you would sink to your knees."

As they drew closer, the small group realized that the foal's dam had lost her battle with marsh mud. Unable to get out, she had died on the scene. The baby, however, was light enough to stay on top of the muck and mire. They knew they had to bring him to safety.

"First, my dad and Mr. Tim from England tried to catch him. But the colt was spry enough to allude them," he said. "We all piled off the boat. William - who was about my age - and I started to chase the pony. Then, William lost his shoes in the mud."

Before long, all seven were out in the marsh, trying to capture the bay pinto colt, who was full of spit and vinegar and raw determination.

"Finally, we made a long trip rope with two people on each end. The foal ran laps around it. He ran into the water and swam around the boat. We corralled him in the water and swam him back to the boat."

Hunter said they didn't want the foal to be in full on panic mode, but they needed to catch him in order to save his life.

Photo Courtesy Hunter Leonard

"The grandmother - who was probably 70 - she and I got on one side of the rope while William's mom and my mom got on the other side. It was so hot," he said, noting that they were getting tired. Playing tag with a foal can be exhausting.

"Finally, he ran right into the rope, tripped and went down. My dad fell on top of him to hold him. We lifted him right onto the boat and he stood there as we sailed home."

Hunter said old-timer, Wesley Bloxom was waiting for them on the shoreline. He believes Bloxom was the head of the pony committee that year. He would make sure the orphan foal was cared for, and he did.

"What a crazy introduction to Chincoteague that was for our friends from England," Hunter said with a laugh. "That day, we named the foal, Captain Morgan because their last name was Morgan.

The pony committee nursed the foal, caring for him in the days leading up to Pony Penning. He was one of three orphan foals that year.

Debbie Ober - who runs the Chincoteague Pony Rescue – was at the auction when the three orphan foals came onto the grounds. Back then, foal tags showed the hip number of the dam. Because "Captain Morgan" had been found with his deceased dam, they knew his hip number.

"I heard them announce that he was an orphan," Debbie said, "And then, I heard hip number 76 and I knew White Hills was his dam. This was my Pony Girl's brother," Debbie said.

Debbie's mare, Pony Girl was a sweet pony, and this orphan colt was similar in markings and appearance.

"Someone was bidding on [the orphan] who I knew would not give it a good home," Debbie said, "so I bid."

After winning the foal, Debbie said she had to call her husband to bring the truck and trailer.

"I had not gone there intending to buy," she said with a laugh.

Photo Courttesy of Debbie Ober

Debbie named the colt, Salty Dawg. Later, Pony Committee chair, Naomi Belton told her the colt had been sired by Rainbow Warrior. That made her love him even more.

"He was wonderful," Debbie said. "He never bucked. He was so easy, and within a week of starting training I was riding him everywhere. He went to [shows at] Tuckahoe, Wild West Days… he went all over with me.

Debbie said, in time, she had to narrow down her herd, and she sold Salty Dawg.

"He went to a lady who had just finished school to work

Photo Courtesy of Debbie Ober

in therapy for kids with disabilities. Now, he is used as a therapy pony," she said. "He is perfect for that!"

The Rasmussen family was at that same Pony Penning auction. They ended up purchasing another of the orphan foals.

"My brother and I decided we were going to get a buyback foal that year so his girls would have a pony on the island," Sara Rasmussen shared. Then she laughed. "But an orphan is an orphan and when they wheeled a trailer with three orphans onto the Carnival Grounds shortly before the auction, well, my sister-in-law couldn't help it. I don't think my nieces even knew she was bidding until far into the sale. Then, they both burst out crying."

Sara's niece Brooke remembers the auction well.

"I was 9 years old when we bought Sailor," she remembered. "We actually met him in a trailer at the auction. There were three orphans that year, all in a red trailer with little orphan labels stuck to their hindquarters. A certain foal named Sailor was sticking his head through the bars to get his nose kissed as he had been taught to do."

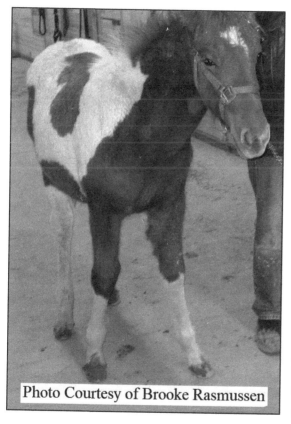

Photo Courtesy of Brooke Rasmussen

Brooke said she had no idea that this little foal would become such a big part of her life, or that he would go on to shape her career choice in the future. On that day, the nine year old, was simply in awe of the fact that they were taking home a real live Chincoteague Pony foal.

Brooke said she was already an avid fan of the book "Misty of Chincoteague." For her, this little chestnut pinto orphan truly was a dream come true.

"We had gone to the auction intending to be mere spectators, as we already had a horse at home. But we fell in love with that little guy almost on sight… and we ended up with a Chincoteague Pony!" Brooke said. "I can safely say he is our favorite impulse buy ever!"

"The horse experience we had up until then was that my parents had ponies growing up and we had a 9-year-old quarter horse at the time. We had no foal experience."

They may not have had foal experience, but where there is a will, there is a way.

"We were very lucky to find a trainer named Julie Arkison, who I still work with today. She helped - and still helps us - with Sailor," Brooke said.

Photo courtesy of Brooke Rasmussen

Brooke said she and her sister, Lauren have been riding Sailor since he was three years old.

"He has been a part of many fun and special memories in his many years with us," she said. "He's a fantastic comic relief to have around."

Brooke said her best memories over the years have had to do with training, and "trying to turn him into a nice, polite, dressage pony."

©Brooke Rasmussen

"Sailor is an energetic and enthusiastic pony who quite likes to push his own agenda," she said. "Sometimes it can be kind of difficult to get him to do something he does not want to do. After months of working with him to trot straight on the rail with his head in a soft position, he finally snorted and lowered his head and did it beautifully for me in the middle of a lesson. It finally felt like I had communicated with him on a different level than we had operated on before."

Brooke said the little orphan that they didn't expect to take home, has been a big influence in her life.

"Sailor has affected my life in so many different ways," she said. "It is because of working with him that I have gained many lifetime skills such as tenacity and patience. He's driven my [desire] to help vulnerable animals," she said. "He is the reason I am currently in law school, working towards a JD specializing in animal law."

Sailor's story - like so many stories that unfold on the island – has had some twists and turns, but it all led to him coming home to the place where he belongs.

Photo Courtesy of Brooke Rasmussen

Pearl – A Rescue Story

On a beautiful day in May of 2016, I was out with friends on a Captain Dan's Around the Island Cruise. There is no guarantee we will find ponies on these incredible pontoon boat cruises, but Captain Dan seldom disappoints, and on this day, he again delivered. As we rounded a long point that jutted out into the bay, we came upon Puzzle's band. That's when I saw Sweet Jane's 2016 filly for the first time.

The evenly marked chestnut pinto clung to her dam's side, the mare that

©2016 Lois Szymanski

some call Duckie. She had the same sweet face as her beautiful dam.

Soaking in the beauty of the moment, I had no idea what was to become of this innocent new foal, or the long hard journey she would face ahead.

I saw the foal again in

July inside the pens on Assateague and again, when they made the swim and came into the carnival grounds on Chincoteague Island.

At auction, I watched to see who was bidding on the filly, and when I saw the buyer going up to the booth to pay, my heart sank. I had concerns about this woman. Too many ponies had died under her care at young ages, including two young studs who were removed from the island, several young mares, and even two studs who had been loaned

©2016 Lois Szymanski

to her for breeding purposes, only to die before returning home. I said a little prayer, hoping I was wrong.

Time passed, and as it is when we are busy with life, Sweet Jane's filly left my thoughts. Then, in April of 2018, I clicked on an online news link about 12 horses that were seized from a property in Rocky Ridge, Maryland. The neighbors had called the county repeatedly over the months, as the owner dragged dead horse after dead horse up into the trees beside their properties. Among the horses and ponies seized, there were several Chincoteague Ponies, and as I leaned in to look at the photo, I recognized Sweet Jane's 2016 filly.

I breathed a sigh of relief that she was alive, and again when I saw that the horses were going to Days End Farm Rescue in Woodbine, Maryland. I knew this operation well. I followed their Facebook page, and had seen several articles on the farm in my local paper. Days End would go to any and all lengths for these horses.

Of the horses seized, two were too weak to survive and died, one with an unborn foal. Two more foals were born out of the surviving mares, and one was in such poor condition, it could not survive. One of the horses, an American Quarter horse, was so weak and emaciated that she had to be supported in a special sling for five weeks. At the time, her caretakes said she was "rapidly declining, emaciated, and suffering from kidney and liver problems due to her depleted state." But she survived, and so did Sweet Jane's beautiful 2016 filly.

The owner was charged with eight counts of animal cruelty and eight additional counts of animal cruelty, and failure to provide nutritious food in sufficient quantities.

In what seemed to me like a slap on the wrist, the owner was granted two years' probation before judgement and ordered to pay more than $1,200 in restitution to Buckeystown Veterinary Hospital for the medical care of the horses. She was allowed to own one therapy animal and will be subject to random check-ins from county officials.

Online, I saw that the vet had deemed the filly a yearling. Her growth had been stunted that much. I stopped to write a note to the rescue, letting them know that she was actually two years old, sending along a photo of her with her dam on the island.

I was not the only one watching Days End Farm Rescue's daily posts and updates. So was Jenna Waybright. She had heard about the case from friends at the barn where she once boarded her gelding.

"When I realized they had Chincoteague ponies, I started emailing back and forth with the rescue," Jenna said, explaining how she had always dreamed of owning a Chincoteague Pony. Her family had been visiting the island for vacations for almost 20 years.

"I really thought it was a shot in the dark," said Jenna. "I never thought they'd let me adopt the young Chincoteague Pony. I knew they were getting a bunch of applications for her, and I just thought it wouldn't be me."

But, lo and behold, Jenna's application was plucked from the stack.

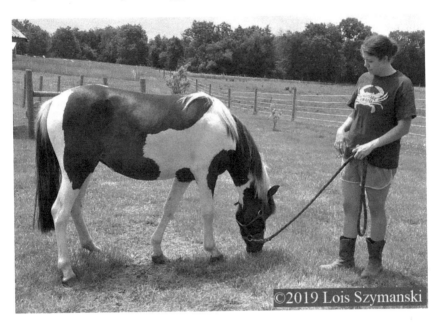

"We went to Days End to meet her a couple times," Jenna said of herself, husband Chris and their children Findley and Burke. "We ended up being a perfect fit, and we became the lucky family [to take home] a two-year old Chincoteague Pony."

At home, the pony they named Pearl fit right in with her two older geldings, Teddy - the middle aged Hanoverian, and Roosevelt – an American Quarter Horse rescued from the kill pens.

"We don't know much of the history of either of our other horses. With Pearl, we were sent pictures of her on the island with her mom. Her first two years were awful, but we know her whole story," Jenna said. "It's really special."

©2019 Lois Szymanski

Jena said few people could understand how she felt when she brought Pearl home.

"I waited more than 15 years to have this breed of pony [that] I'd always dreamed of," she said. "It was like winning the lottery."

Jenna said she had always said, *never another mare*, but that is just what she got in Pearl

"She is the exact picture of a pony mare. She is spunky. She is smart. She loves to have fun," Jenna said. "Sometimes we run with her up and down the fence line as if we are racing. She's the first to figure out new things like our new automatic waterer, and she's bold. She doesn't seem to let her first two years affect this new life she has."

Since Pearl came home, Jenna and her husband have delivered a third child, another baby boy that they named Carter.

"I think I have a greater appreciation for her personality since the boys outnumber the girls in our house," she said with a laugh. "It's like the girls have to stick together."

According to Jenna, Pearl has exceeded their expectations, and as she heads off to a trainer this week, she believes the mare will continue to please. The kids love her, too, but mostly her daughter, Burke.

"Burke especially loves her," Jenna said. "We are decorating her big girl room all in ponies. Burke can't wait to ride her when she comes back from training. Every stuffed animal she owns is named Pearl. They all love their Pearl girl!"

Jenna said she hopes, after training, they will have a kid's pony.

"We hope she and the kids can grow up together," she said.
Pearl's story has an ending that we wish for every pony that leaves the Chincoteague Wildlife Refuge, the best kind of life!

©2020 Jenna Waybright

Muddy Mayli & More

One warm evening, Darcy Cole joined Hunter Leonard and his wife, Rebekah and me as we sat down to talk ponies. Hunter is always great about sharing stories and at handling my constant questions. He has the same tolerance that his father, Arthur and his grandfather, Donald showed me during the early years of my writing career, when they often met with me for interviews.

I asked Hunter if he remembered the time that Kachina's Mayli Mist got stuck in the mud. Hearing about this scary episode stood out among my 2015 memories. He nodded, and Darcy reminded me that this was just after Mayli had bonded with Pixie. The two young mares were seen together frequently during that time period.

After he saw Mali flailing in the mud, it was Captain Dan who called it in.

"We sailed up there, me and Luke, Alex and Sam and another cowboy," Hunter said. "She was almost into the water, but had hit some really bad mud. Bobby [Lapin] came up there on the gator and met us there. She was at the edge of the marsh, near the water. The tide had fallen, and you could see that she had thrashed around so long that she was exhausted."

The palomino pinto didn't have the energy she needed to get herself out of the thick, heavy marsh mud, and Hunter explained why.

"Ponies have a harder time because their hooves are so narrow. The more they push down the more their feet keep going down," he said.

"We were dumbfounded about how we were going to get her out. It was getting pretty dark, and eventually, we rolled her out. The way we do it, is we tie a rope to the gator, put her in a heavy duty tarp and wrap the tarp all the way over her, like a taco.

©2015 Lois Szymanski

The gator acts like a sled, pulling her across the marsh. We got her out to the road and to the trailer and once she got on hard surface she could stand up."

Hunter said the pony committee has had their share of ponies stuck in the mud, but this one was particularly difficult. Still, they got it done, and amazingly, the sweet pinto still had enough strength to get to her feet.

"We get these calls every year, for ponies stuck in the marsh," Hunter said. It's usually up in that section where Puzzle's band stays. Up there all the edges are made of rib mussels, which kind of keep it together and the edges are always hard. You'll notice, if you go up there, you'll see that they [the ponies] only stay around the edges where it is hard, not further in. They know where they need to stay."

Hunter said in 2015, after Dunkaroo – aka Lily – was rescued, the foal had to be rescued again. (The first rescue story is in Volume II of Chincoteague Pony Tales.)

"We were like, here we go again," Hunter said. "The foal had been napping and when she got up, she tried to go her mother, Gidget. The marsh is kind of like a U, and she tried to cut across. That's where she'd gotten stuck in a [muddy] ditch.

"Me and Bobby [Lapin's] son Justin were out there that day. We went up, gut after gut after gut. It's at least a half a mile up the road. After we got her out, we just wanted to get her to drink. But she wouldn't drink, and she wouldn't follow us. After a bit, finally, Puzzle's band worked their way back to them."

Lily/ Dunkaroo - 2016

Hunter spoke of the mud found in the northern compartment, much more than found in the southern acres.

"There is some pretty bad territory up there for a pony," he said. "It took us a long time to get her out. This is why we keep the fall pickup foals south until they get more mature and get to know the land. We get two or three calls every year for ponies up there stuck in the mud."

Not all the calls the pony committee gets are for ponies stuck in the marsh, though.

"There was another time, a couple of years ago when Darcy had called," Hunter said. "Wild Thing was limping pretty bad. So, I went up in the boat and the others went up in trucks. His band is so far north. They didn't know how they would get him back, because this is like, six miles from the corral, way north. That's too far for them to go."

Hunter said that's when the group had the idea to build a corral right there.

"They had the idea of running a rope around the trees in about a hundred foot section."

©2019 Lois Szymanski

He laughed when he noted how quickly they realized this would not work for a smart stallion like Wild Thing.

"It's off topic, but that Wild Thing is so smart," Hunter said, shaking his head. "When he goes through the chute at roundup [for shots and worming] you can bet on what he will do. He hates it, so he goes straight down - his belly on the ground - as soon as he goes in chute. There's so little space in there, but he does it. He crouches low. Then it takes 20 minutes to get him up. He hates shots and he's so smart."

"When we knew the rope corral wouldn't work, we decided we'd just leave him and come the next day. But he was fine when they went back the next day. We think he probably had an abscess."

Hoof abscesses occur when bacteria is trapped between the sensitive laminae - the tissue layer that bonds the hoof capsule to the coffin bone -

and the hoof wall. The bacteria causes a thick pus, which builds up, putting pressure on the hoof wall. It can be extremely painful, but then, when the abscess pops and the pus drains out there is almost immediate relief.

Hunter remembered a time when Starry Night had a likely hoof abscess.

"She was very pregnant at the time, and limping awful, really bad," he said. "Early one morning, before work, I sailed my boat up Black Duck Drain and there she was, just standing along the edge with Riptide. I could tell she was in pain. Normally, I would never do this, but she was so calm, I just walked up and petted her a little bit, very calm. I was very wary. They can cow-kick you at any minute and can break a leg, and I was by myself, but I thought, she is pretty calm, I am going to feel her legs. So, I went all up and down her legs. On the one, I saw that she had an abscess in the fetlock. It was noticeably hotter, and it was hard. You could tell it was an abscess. Even though after an abscess pops, they are usually fine, you still worry about infection."

©2017 Lois Szymanski

Hunter said they were having excessive heat at the time, so they didn't want to round the herd up. Instead, later in the day, he went back with his dad, Arthur Leonard.

"We went up this one little drain and I got out with a bucket full of vet supplies. I was going to give her a shot of penicillin so there would be no infection. I loaded 10 ccs and walked up to her with my gloves on. But I had waders on and they made a little noise. I would get right up next to her and she would run away. I tried so many times, like 10 or 15 times. She got farther and farther away, until we had to quit."

Hunter said, even without the shot, Starry did just fine. The abscess likely popped, because she healed right up, as they often do. With salty soaks, sun and sky, sometimes nature offers just what the pony needs.

These are just a few examples of how members of the fire company's pony committee are always there. Whenever they hear a wild pony is in need they show up, volunteering their time and compassion on a regular basis. The next time you see a saltwater cowboy, stop to thank him if you get the chance. They take care of the ponies we love so we can love them for another day… and another and another.

©2014 Lois Szymanski

Afterword & Acknowledgements

Flowing manes and tails catch the wind and billow like rippling flags. It stops you in your tracks. From velvety mare muzzles to whiskery foal chins, everything about these graceful and glorious wild and free ponies sucks us in and makes us love them. Thank you, Chincoteague Pony friends, for always encouraging me to collect and share their tales. I could not do this without a lot of help, and I have a lot of folks to thank.

Thank you first to members of the Chincoteague Volunteer Fire Company and the staff and volunteers of the Chincoteague National Wildlife Refuge. Without your watchful eyes and loving hands, the ponies would not be here for us to enjoy. Thank you, Pony Committee for the hours and hours of volunteer service. You keep them safe and strong and always have their well-being in mind. It means so much to all of us - hundreds of thousands of admirers, worldwide.

Thank you to everyone who shared their tales and their photos for this book. Names are noted with each story and photo.

A special thanks to Hunter Leonard for sitting down with me again and again to share the stories and details I crave. My constant questions are a lot to handle, but you always manage them with a willing smile. And to your wife, Rebekah, whose heart and extra input is like icing on the cake.

Heartfelt thanks also to Darcy Cole for the hundreds of miles hiked annually to check on the herds and for keeping us informed, always offering that extra pair of eyes on the ponies we love. Because of your vigilance and the reports that you make, more than one pony's life has been saved. Extra deep gratitude to both Darcy and Steve Cole for always willingly sharing your photos with me.

I also want to thank Captain Dan of Captain Dan's Around the Island Cruises for taking me to see my first pony swim from a boat, for always answering my crazy questions without hesitation, for making regular pony reports on your page and for making that call to report a pony in danger time and time again. You mean so much to all of us.

I also want to thank Debbie Ober and the Chincoteague Pony Rescue for offering a safe landing spot for Chincoteague Ponies in need, and for answering my questions when I come to call.

And to everyone who loves these ponies and shares your stories online, you inspire me daily. We truly are one great big family of pony-lovers, and that is a support system worth its weight in gold.

Helpful Links

Chincoteague Chamber of Commerce   www.chincoteaguechamber.com

Chincoteague Volunteer Fire Company   https://cvfc3.com

Chincoteague Pony Rescue   www.chincoteagueponyrescue.org

Chincoteague Tourism   www.chincoteague.com

The Feather Fund   www.featherfund.net

Find These Helpful Facebook Pages

I Love Chincoteague Ponies   *   The Chincoteague Legacy Group

Bands of the Wild Chincoteague Pony Herds   *   DSC Photography

Chincoteague Pony Rescue   *   Captain Dan's Around the Island Tours

The Chincoteague Pony Pedigree Database   *   The Feather Fund

Chincoteague Pony Class of (fill in the year)